Hot Chilli, Cold Chilli
The Chilli Cook Book

Sarah Thompson

To order additional copies of this book, contact:
Xlibris
0800-056-3182
www.xlibrispublishing.co.uk
Orders@ Xlibrispublishing.co.uk

DEDICATIONS

This book is dedicated firstly to my Mum... Who passed away in February 2018.
For inviting me in to her kitchen as a young child and, imparting her
culinary knowledge to me, which has lasted me a life time
I still love to cook, bake and create in my kitchen.

And to Steve Cooley and Shawn Overthrow, whom, with out their sauces, rubs
and chutney's this book wouldn't of been written, Thank you so much Guy's.

And to my wonderful partner John, for all the love and support that you
have given me and help in creating some of these recipes

And whilst writing this cook book,
you haven't minded being my chief tester and tried something new I've created...

Photo Pascal Le Grand

Photo by Pascal Le Grand

A BRIEF HISTORY OF THE CHILLI

Chillies originated in Mexico and first traded around 6000 years ago,
they have been part of the human diet since 7000BC.

Chillies were grown around the world from around 1493
commercially and used in medicine from 1494.

Many cultivars spread across the world and are used in both food and traditional medicine ...

Peru is considered to have the highest cultivated capsicum diversity...
Although you can find chilli peppers almost anywhere in the world...

There are 5 species and cultivars
Capsicum annum :
Bell peppers, wax, cayenne, jalapeños

Capsicum frutescens :
Tabasco,Thai peppers, piri piri.

Capsicum chinense :
Naga, habanero, Scotch Bonnet.

Capsicum pubescens :
Rocoto peppers.

Capsicum baccatum :
Aji peppers.

THE SCOVILLE SCALE
FOR MEASURING THE HEAT OF CHILLI PEPPERS

15,000,000 Pure Capsaicin

2,000,000 Pepper spray

1,400,000-2,000,000 Carolina Reaper

1,200,000-2,000,000 Trinidad Scorpion

855,001,041,427 Ghost Pepper

425,000-577,000 Chocolate Habanero

100,000-350,000 Habanero

100,000-350,000 Scotch Bonnet

50,000-100-000 Thai Pepper

30,000-50,000 Cayenne Pepper

30,000-50,000 Tabasco Pepper

10,000-20,000 Serrano Pepper

5,000-10,000 Hungarian Hot Wax

2,500-8,000 Jalapeño Pepper

100-500 Pimento Pepper

0 Bell Pepper

Anatomy of a Chilli

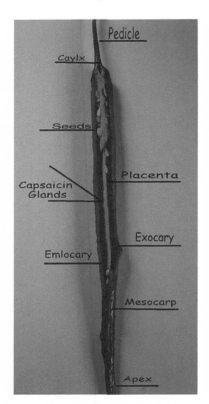

INTENSITY

The substance which gives chilli peppers their pungency (spicy heat) it is called 'capsaicin' (methyl-I-N-vanillyl-6-nonenamide)... These are collectively called 'capsaicinoids' The amount of capsaicin can vary by variety and growing conditions... A water stressed plant can have much hotter chilli pepper pods, than one well looked after.

When eating chilli peppers, the capsaicin binds with the pain receptors in your mouth and throat, evoking pain, via spinal and nerve relaying to the brain stem and thalamus, this is where the heat and discomfort are perceived...

The heat of the chilli pepper is measured by the 'Scoville Heat Units' (SHU) From '0' to '2.2' million SHU.

Notable Hot Chilli Peppers
CAROLINA REAPER 2.2M SHU
TRINIDAD MORUGA SCORPION 2.0M SHU
BHUT JOLOKIA (GHOST PEPPER) 1.58M SHU
TRINIDAD SCORPION BUTCH T. 1.463M SHU
NAGA VIPER 1.4M SHU

- - - - -

Capsaicin is acidic so can be neutralized with an alkaline i.e. yoghurt, milk, cream...

- - - - -

CULINARY USES

Chilli pepper pods, which are actually berries, can be used fresh or dried...
Chilli peppers can be preserved for a long time...
They can be dried, ground in to powder, smoked, pickled...
And of course fresh in many dishes.
As you will see throughout this chilli cook book...

Red chilli peppers contain large amounts of vitamin C and they are also a good source of beta-Carotene they are also a good source of vitamin B6.

MEDICINAL USES

Capsaicin, the chemical in chilli peppers and which makes them hot... It is used as an analgesic, in topical ointments, nasal sprays, and dermal patches to relive pain...

There are 3 primary spellings of the word 'chilli'
chilli... Which I use.
chili
chile

CONVERSION TABLES
APPROXIMATE LIQUID CONVERSIONS

METRIC	IMPERIAL	AUS.	USA.
50ml	2fl oz	¼ cup	¼ cup
125ml	4fl oz	½ cup	½ cup
175ml	6fl oz	¾ cup	¾ cup
225ml	8fl oz	1 cup	1 cup
300ml	10fl oz / ½ pint	½ pint	1 ¼ cups
450ml	16fl oz	2 cups	2 cups / 1 pint
600ml	20fl oz/ 1 pint	1 pint	2 ½ cups
1 litre	35fl oz/1 ¾ pints	1 ¾ pints	1 quart

ml = millilitre, oz = ounce, fl. oz = fluid ounce

OVEN CONVERSION TABLES

GAS	C	FAN	F	OVEN TEMPERATURE
Quarter	110	90	225	VERY COOL
Half	120	100	250	VERY COOL
1	140	120	275	COOL or SLOW
2	150	130	300	COOL or SLOW
3	160	140	325	WARM
4	180	160	350	MODERATE
5	190	170	375	MODERATELY HOT
6	**200**	180	400	FAIRLY HOT
7	**220**	200	425	HOT
8	**230**	210	450	VERY HOT
9	**240**	220	475	VERY HOT

SPOON MEASUREMENTS

◊ Spoon measurements are level unless otherwise specified
◊ 1 teaspoon = 5ml. 1 tablespoon = 15ml

CONVERSION TABLE

oz -(ounces / pounds) to g -(grams) and k – (kilo)

OUNCE - oz	GRAMS - g
½ oz	15 g
1oz	25g
2oz	50g
3oz	75g
4oz	100g
5oz	125g
6oz	150g
7oz	175g
8oz	200g
9oz	225g
10oz	250g
15oz	375g
20oz	500g
25oz	625g
30oz	750g
40oz	1000g / 1 k.

Contents

GLOSSARY

Cook- Cooking time

(DCSauce) Daddy Cool's Sauce

Prep. Preparation time

(V) Vegetarian

g- gram

oz. ounce

Photo by Pascal Le Grand

STARTER, BROTHS, MARINADES, SAUCES & SOUPS

SPICY FISH ROLLS

Makes 8-10
Prep. 20 mins. Cook 5-8 mins per batch

1 tin sardines in tomato sauce
1 egg
3 tsp garlic powder
2 tsp Smokey Chipotle Jam (DC Sauce)
12 Chinese pancakes
1 cup / 225ml. sunflower oil

HOW to COOK

◊ Bone out sardines, put in a bowl, add jam.
◊ Using a fork, break up fish and stir until evenly combined.
◊ Crack egg in to another bowl, and whisk up, until frothy
◊ Take 1 pancake, brush all over with egg.

Add 1 tabsp. of the fish mixture, place in the centre of the pancake, roughly form into a sausage shape.

◊ Fold pancake in half, fold in ends, roll in to spring roll shape.
◊ THE EGG 'GLUES' THE ROLLS TOGETHER..
◊ Continue to use all the mixture and pancakes
◊ Heat oil, in a wok or large frying pan.
◊ Take a small piece of pancake, drop it carefully in the oil, when it starts to fry vigorously, Carefully start to add 4 pancakes at a time.
◊ Fry for 3-5 minutes turning as needed or until golden brown all over.
◊ Place on some kitchen towel, to drain off excess oil.
◊ Keep first batch in a warm oven (gas3) add the rest.
◊ Serve HOT.
◊ Good with fried rice or noodles.

The idea for spicy noodles came from needing something quick and spicy for lunch one day... it takes 5-8 minutes to make, it's hot and you can make it as hot and spicy as you like... Great served with prawn crackers...

SPICY NOODLES

Serves 2-4

2 packs dried noodles (59g)
½ pint boiled water
1 medium onion
1 chicken stock cube
1 tsp Henry's steak rub
2 tabsp. sweet chilli sauce
1 heaped tsp cornflour + 2 tabsp cold water, mixed

HOW to COOK

◊ In a large pan place noodles, broken up and add the ½ pint of water.
◊ Add the stock cube, stir until dissolved
◊ Finely sliced the onion and add to the pan
◊ Add the steak powder and chilli sauce and stir.
◊ Bring to the boil stir every few minutes.
◊ Noodles will be soft after 5 minutes
◊ Serve hot …

MARINADE FOR CHICKEN, BEEF or PORK

Serves 2
Prep. 30 mins. 4-6 hrs. marinating Cook 45 mins.

1 chicken breast, 6oz beef or pork, thinly sliced
1 onion, diced
2 tabsp. chilli honey (The Little Chilli Shop) (or honey of your choice)
2 tabsp. hoisin sauce
4 tabsp. dark soy sauce
2 tabsp. passata
½ pint + 4 tsp. cold water
2 tsp. cornflour

HOW to COOK

◊ Lightly fry the onion until caramelized, let cool, (10 mins.)
◊ Place all ingredients in a oven proof dish
◊ Mix together
◊ Add your meat, coat all pieces of the meat with the marinade
◊ Marinade for 4-6 hours, covered, on the bottom shelf of the fridge.
◊ Remove from fridge 1 hour from cooking to bring back up to room temperature
◊ Heat oven to gas 5
◊ Place the oven proof dish in centre of the oven
◊ Cook for 30 to 40 minutes, or until the meat is lightly browned
◊ To thicken the sauce, add cornflour mixture, stir in well, return to the oven for 5 minutes, then remove from the oven stir well again.
◊ Serve HOT, with egg fried rice or mixed seasonal vegetables.

TIP

Using cornflour to thicken sauces.

Mix the cornflour with COLD water to a smooth paste, and add it to the sauce, combine well. Cook for 5 minutes, before serving.

'XXX' LAMB, CHICKEN OR BEEF, MARINADE.

Serves 2
Prep. 20 mins. Cook 5-10 mins.

500g Lamb, Chicken or Beef, cut in to strips
8 fl. oz. Apple Cider Vinegar
1 tabsp. XXX BadBoy (DC Sauces)
Salt and Pepper to taste...
2oz Plain Flour
500ml Sunflower Oil (for deep frying)
Batter mix (See N.B at base of page)

HOW to COOK

◊ Cut your chosen meat in to thin strips, place in a glass dish and set as side.
◊ Mix together the cider vinegar and XXX sauce, pour over the meat.
◊ Cover in cling-film, place on bottom shelf of the fridge over night...
◊ Remove from fridge and hour before cooking to bring meat up to room temperature.
◊ Place the plain flour on a flat plate
◊ An make the batter, in a large bowl...
◊ Heat the cooking oil in a large frying pan or wok on high heat...
◊ Take a strip of meat roll it in the flour then dip into the batter and then fry...
◊ Cook until golden brown, 4 -5 minutes
◊ Cook 8 -10 pieces at a time
◊ Drain off excess oil on kitchen towel...
◊ Eat HOT with dips and salad...

N.B.
Batter Mix
8oz Plain Flour
2 medium Eggs
½ pint Full fat Milk..
Whisk all together in a large bowl...

SPICY CHICKEN or VEGETABLE SAUCE (V)

1 x chicken or vegetable stock cube
½ pt. water (cold)
Tabsp. madras powder
½ tsp. mixed spice powder (DCSauce)
1 ½ tsp light brown sugar
1 ½ tabsp. balsamic vinegar
1 tabsp. lemon juice
½ tsp garlic powder
(2 tsp. cornflour, 4 tsp. cold water mixed together, to thicken)

HOW to COOK

◊   Place all ingredients in a medium size pan, except the cornflour, stir well, together.
◊   Bring to boil, keep stirring.
◊   Add the cornflour, stir all ingredients together
◊   Simmer for 10 minutes... Turn off heat...
◊   Can be used straight away as a sauce or left to cool and used as a marinade.

You could replace the chicken stock cube with a vegetable as this works well too !

HENRY'S ORCHARD SPICED – CHICKEN BROTH

I created this delicious broth, slightly sweet in flavour but, works so well with the chicken... serve with prawn crackers
Great for on a cold day...

HENRY'S ORCHARD SPICED – CHICKEN BROTH

For two servings, main course, or 4 servings as an hors d'oeuvres
Serves 2-4
Prep. 15-20 mins Cook 20 mins

1pt. cold water
2 chicken stock cubes
4 tabsp. Orchard Spiced sauce (Henry's)
1 small onion, thinly sliced
1 chicken breast, lightly roasted and shredded
2oz/ 50g dessicated coconut
3 heaped tabsp. soft brown sugar
2oz / 50g frozen mixed vegetables or fresh
2oz /50g. Chinese egg noodles

HOW to COOK

- ◊ In a large pan, add the water, 2 stock cubes, and chilli sauce.
- ◊ Combine together... Bring to the boil, on a high heat.
- ◊ Add the onion, noodles and shredded chicken and vegetables and coconut, stir well, to combine all ingredients together.
- ◊ Reduce heat to simmer for 10 minutes
- ◊ Serve hot
- ◊ Can be served as a hors d'oeuvres or main course.

TIP:

You can add less or more chilli sauce, depending on how hot you like it.

4 tablespoons is medium to hot...

CHICKEN & LENTIL BROTH, WITH A TWIST...

SERVES 4
Prep. 20 mins. Cook 20 mins.

250ml passata (1 carton)
½ pint cold water
1 chicken stock cube
½ tsp. sea salt
1 onion, sliced
1 cooked chicken breast, lightly roasted (20-25 mins.) shredded, with 2 forks
4oz/ 100g x red lentils – pre-soaked and drained. *
10-12 twists masala curry salt (DCSauce)
¼ tsp Ghost Pepper Extreme XXX (DCSauce)

HOW to COOK

◊   Place the passata, water, onion and masala salt and XXX sauce, in a large pan
◊   Bring to boil, then boil for 10 minutes
◊   Stirring regularly
◊   Tear up the chicken breast and add this to the soup, add the pre-soaked lentils
◊   Leave to boil for 5 mins
◊   Reduce to a simmer
◊   Serve hot...
◊   Garnish with chopped chives
◊   Ideal for a winters day lunch, serve with crusty bread.

N.B.

Soak the red lentils for 2 hours before use, drain before adding to the soup....

Well, I said I like to create new dishes, so I have...

I wanted something different to gravy, something quite thick but, hot,spicy and lot's of flavour and this is what I came up with... This is the result

CHILLI LAGER SAUCE

Prep. 10 mins. Cook 10 mins.

½ can of any lager
2-3 tabsps. Salt
1 x chicken stock cube
½ tsp. chilli paste, any heat or flavour (your choice)
2tsp cornflour plus 3 tsp cold water,(mixed together)
5 tabsps. caramel sauce
2 tabsps. Tomato ketchup

HOW to COOK

A very easy and quick recipe...All in one pan...

◊ Place all ingredients in a large pan, bring to a simmer
◊ Simmer for 5 minutes
◊ Now add the cornflour mixture to thicken the sauce..
◊ Simmer for another 5 minutes
◊ Use this sauce HOT !
◊ As a dipping sauce, for chips/fries or chicken goujons, tortilla wraps, etc.

MAIN COURSES

A very tasty recipe... Lot's of flavours happening and they all work so well together !

This is a Mexican style main dish or can be a starter...

The smokey chipotle rub, setting the scene and, the strong cider bringing all the flavours to the fore and presenting in a rounded flavour, in a dish fun to eat...

CHICKEN WAT'S IT'S NAME

serves 2
Prep. 20 mins plus marinating time. Cook 20 mins.

2 chicken breasts
½ pint/300ml strong still cider
2 tabsps. Tomato sauce
3 tabsps smokey chipotle rub (DCSauce)
1 chicken stock cube
1 tabsp. light brown sugar
1 tsp. dark soy sauce
1 tsp cornflour
sea salt & pepper to taste
 4 tabsps. sunflower oil for cooking
2 potions of stir fry vegetables

HOW to COOK

◊ Dice the chicken in to bite size pieces, place them on a plate and sprinkle with the rub and half the cider on both sides of the chicken, cover the dish with cling film and set a side for up to 4 hours... Or over night.
◊ Remove the chicken from the dish, saving as much of the marinade stock as possible.
◊ Using a wok or large frying pan, add the cooking oil and heat on high for 1 minute, then add the chicken and cook until lightly browned.
◊ Once cooked, remove the chicken from the pan, remove around half the oil, re-heat the oil add stir fry vegetables
◊ Once the vegetables are cooked set aside
◊ Using a sieve, strain the marinade and stock and bring to the boil.
◊ Add the rest of the cider, tomato sauce and cornflour, bring back to the boil
◊ Add the sugar, to make a thick smooth paste.
◊ Pour over the chicken and vegetables and serve hot...

CHICKEN 'WAT'S IT'S NAME'

CHIPOTLE CUBED SPUDS

Serves 2-3
Prep. 10 mins. Cook 40 mins.

1Lb potatoes...
1 cup olive oil
3 tsp. smokey chipotle rub (DC Sauce)
1 Litre peanut or rapeseed oil... For deep frying

HOW to COOK

◊   Peel and cut the potatoes in to cubes. Boil for 15 minutes
◊   Heat oven to Gas 5
◊   Drain and dry thoroughly
◊   Heat the oil in a large pan on a high heat, then fry the potatoes until golden and crispy..
◊   Drain off excess oil, and place in an oven proof dish, keep the fried potatoes hot in the oven... 15 mins.
◊   You may need to cook the potatoes in batches.
◊   Remove all the potatoes from the oven at the last minute, toss in the olive oil and sprinkle with the Chipotle rub... be quick...
◊   Then place the coated potatoes back in the oven for 5 minutes
◊   Serve this dish HOT ! .

SPICY DEVIL'S TANDOORI CHICKEN

Serves 2

2 large chicken breast fillet, diced
1 onion
8 closed cup mushrooms, sliced
1 tub passata
3 tabsp. tomato puree

Marinade

1 tsp. tandoori paste
6 tabsp, tomato ketchup
½ pint cold water
1 tsp mild paprika

HOW to COOK

◊ Dice and marinate the chicken, put on one side for 4-6 hours or over night, on the bottom shelf of the fridge.
◊ If using the next day, remove from fridge, and hour before cooking, so that the ingredients are at room temperature.
◊ Heat oven to Gas 5, 375F
◊ Slice the onions and mushrooms, lightly fry, drain off oil. Set a side.
◊ In a large oven proof dish, place in the chicken, onions and mushrooms, and all the other ingredients, stir together...
◊ Place the oven proof dish on a tray, in the centre of the oven, cover with tin foil for 35 minutes, then remove for the last 15 minutes.
◊ Stir a few times.
◊ Serve hot, with boiled or fried rice and chapatis.

The Marinade:

◊ tomato ketchup, tandoori paste, paprika and water.
◊ Mix all ingredients together, pour over the chicken, mix all together, cover with cling-film, leave to one side.

BOSTON, BAKED BEANS (V)

Serves 4
Prep. 20 mins. Cook 2hrs 5 mins. With tinned beans 35 mins.

400g/ 14oz dried haricot or 5 bean mix, or 1 tin mixed beans,
1 large onion
4 slices thick-cut smoked bacon (leave out for vegetarian option)
3 tabsp. maple syrup or black treacle
40g/ 1½oz soft brown sugar
1 tsp. Henry's 'No Smoke Without Fire' sauce... Or any medium heat sauce of your choice
900ml/1½ pints beef stock or vegetable stock
Salt and black pepper to taste...
1 tabsp. sunflower oil

HOW to COOK

◊ Place beans in a large bowl, pour over enough cold water to cover them and leave to soak over night...
◊ Drain the beans and rinse thoroughly with cold water. Place the beans in a large saucepan, cover with fresh water and bring to the boil... Boil vigorously for 10 minutes...
◊ Preheat the oven to 200C/400F/Gas 6...
◊ Peel and slice the onion, cut the bacon in to cubes, lightly fry the onion and bacon, for 2-3 minutes, stirring, until the onion are transparent, and the bacon is starting to brown...
◊ Drain the beans and place them in a large ovenproof dish add the onions and bacon... Stir in the maple syrup, sugar, mustard and stock, and season with salt and pepper...
◊ Cover the dish with a lid or tin foil, Bake for 1½ hours, or until all the liquid is absorbed...and the beans are tender... Stir well from time to time...
◊ Remove lid or tin foil 30 minutes before the end of cooking..
◊ Check the seasoning and more if needed.
◊ Serve HOT!

COOKING TIP

Make sure the beans do not dry out... Add a little more water or stock, if needed...

DO NOT Add extra salt until the end of cooking and this will make the beans hard and very salty to taste...

ABOUT THIS RECIPE

This recipe is in honour of one of my chilli guru's David Flipp, from Boston MA, USA...

For the American readers of this book, you can use any of Boston Ballistic sauces for these recipes Thanks David... email and website on supplier's page.

JOLOKIA CHICKEN BITES

Serves 2
Prep. 25 mins Cook 10-12 mins.

2 eggs, beaten
4 tabsp. cornflour
4 tabsp. self raising flour
1 level tsp. Sea Salt
2 tsp. garlic powder
2 chicken breasts (dried)... See Notes at base of page. (N.B.)
1 tsp. Jolokia sauce (or to taste)... (D C Sauces)
1 cup sunflower oil

HOW to COOK.

◊ Crack the eggs in to a bowl and whisk together.
◊ Add chilli sauce, salt,garlic powder and whisk all together and combine evenly
◊ Finely chop the dried chicken
◊ Add the chicken to the egg mixture – and stir in until covered.
◊ Sift in cornflour and self-raising flour (at this point the mixture will start to thicken up)
◊ If the mixture does not stiffen up then add a little more self-raising flour
◊ Heat the oil, scoop out a heaped tabsp. of the mixture and ease it in to the oil, carefully so you don't get splashed (use two spoons)
◊ Flatten each spoonful of mixture with a spatula, cook 4 to 6 at a time.
◊ Cook for 4-5 minutes, to cook through, turning regularly
◊ Cut the first patty in half to check it is cooked and heated right through, if not return to the pan and cook for a few more minutes.
◊ The patties should be golden brown
◊ Place on kitchen towel to soak up any excess oil.
◊ Serve hot or cold, with rice or salad and dips....

TIPS

◊   When shallow frying if the outside of the food seems to darken very quickly, but the inside is still raw, then the oil is to **HOT !** - Turn down the heat and remove the pan from the ring for 5 minutes and add a little more <u>cold</u> oil, pour in slowly.

◊   Return the pan to the ring and carry on cooking the patties.

N.B.

The dried chicken in this recipe is simply leftovers from a roast chicken, that has been dried out in a low oven gas 3, for 30 minutes and then left to go cold.

Moist chicken will not work in this recipe....

CHILLI BBQ PORK

Serves 2
Prep. 10 mins. Cook 15 mins

2 pork loin chops, cut in to strips
2 onions, sliced
4 mushroom, sliced
1 tabsp. Henry's BBQ Rub
250ml passata
1 tabsp. hoisin sauce
2 tabsp. light brown sugar
½ pint boiled water
1 tsp. cornflour
2 tabsp. sunflower oil

HOW to COOK

- ◊ Heat the oil in a large frying pan or wok
- ◊ Fry off the pork, when seared all over add the sliced vegetables.
- ◊ As soon as the onions are translucent, sprinkle over the BBQ rub.
- ◊ Dry fry on a high heat for 4 -5 minutes
- ◊ Then turn the heat down to medium.
- ◊ Add water to de-glaze the pan.
- ◊ Add the passata and combine the mixture together.
- ◊ Mix the cornflour with the cold water, and stir in to the dish.
- ◊ Keep stirring until the mixture thickens.
- ◊ Add a tabsp. of Hoisin sauce and stir thoroughly
- ◊ Serve hot, with Sarah's Egg Fried Rice or plain boiled rice.

AROMATIC, CHICKEN, LENTIL & BEAN CURRY...

SERVES 4
Prep. 2 ½ hrs. Cook 25 minutes

4 chicken breast
250ml passata (1 carton)
1 pint chicken stock
1 onion, sliced
4oz/75g red lentils – pre-soaked and drained. *
4oz/75g - 5 Bean Soup Mix, Soaked and boiled until soft...*
1 tsp 'Ketch the Reaper (DCSauce)
2 tsp Middle Eastern Rub (Henry's)
3 tsp Cornflour and 4 tabsp. cold water to mix.
1" Grated Fresh Ginger Root (optional)

HOW to COOK

◊   Place the passata, chicken stock, onion, (ginger) in a large pan
◊   Bring to boil, then boil for 10 minutes, stirring regularly
◊   Add the pre-soaked lentils and beans
◊   Let boil for 5 mins
◊   Reduce to a simmer
◊   Add the rub and reaper sauce, stir all together...
◊   Add the cornflour, stir in simmer for 2-3 minutes
◊   Serve hot... With chapatis (see page 64)

N.B. *

Soak the red lentils for **2** hours before use, drain and wash, before adding to the curry....

Soak for **2** hours and boil the 5 beans soup mix for 15 minutes, and drain, before adding to the curry...
DO NOT ADD ANY SALT, as this will make the beans go hard...

This curry is better made the day before eating, to bring out the best flavour...

FRAGRANT MIXED VEGETABLE CHOW MEIN (V)

Serves 2
Prep. 15 mins. Cook 40 mins.

3 medium potatoes
1 onion
2oz/25g peas 2oz/25g mushrooms
2 tabsp. Henry's 'No Smoke Without Fire' sauce
2 level tsp garlic powder
2 level tsp fenugreek powder
4 tabsp. sweet chilli sauce
1 tabsp. dark soy sauce
½ pint cold water
2-3 tabsp. cooking oil
2 potions of spaghetti or egg noodles

HOW to COOK

◊ Put 2 pints of cold water in a large pan, bring to the boil and place in the spaghetti, bring back to the boil and cook until al dente
◊ Slice and dice the potatoes and onions and mushrooms
◊ Heat the oil in a large pan or wok, on a high heat.
◊ Add the diced potatoes and fry for 2-3 minutes
◊ Add the onions and fry for 2-3 minutes
◊ Add the peas and spices and the water, (As no one likes fried peas).
◊ Turn the heat down and cover the pan, simmer for 10-15 minutes.
◊ Now add the spaghetti, cook for a further 5-10 minutes
◊ Stir regularly
◊ Serve this dish hot, with Prawn Crackers...

GOLDEN CURRY – BASE (V)

Serves 3-4
Prep. 10 mins. Cook 10-15 mins.

2 cups red lentils... pre-soaked and drained
2 onions, finely sliced
2 cloves of garlic, finely sliced
2oz/50g raisins or sultanas
2 tsp madras powder (heaped)
½ tsp turmeric
2 tsp of matured ' Ketch the Reaper' Chilli sauce...(DC Sauce) *
2 tabsp sunflower oil
1 tsp mixed herbs (dried)
½ pint passata
½ pint cold water
3 tsp cornflour, mixed with 2 tabsp. cold water...

HOW to COOK

◊　Heat the oil in a wok or frying pan
◊　Add the onions and garlic, lightly fry, until soft
◊　Add the mixed herbs and passata and combine together
◊　Add the madras powder, fenugreek powder and the ground turmeric... stir
◊　Take off the heat... Add the red lentils and return to the heat... Stir well..
◊　Add a little cold water if necessary, as the lentils may soak up all the liquid
◊　Add the 'Ketch the Reaper' Stir in well
◊　Bring to the boil add the cornflour and the sultanas or raisins and stir well again...
◊　Reduce the heat and simmer for 5 minutes, or until the curry has thickened up...
◊　Serve with rice and chaptis

You can add Beef, Chicken, Fish, Pork or Vegetables to this dish...

NOTE :

Adding brown sugar to this base curry, will regulate the flavour and temperature.
This depends on your personal tastes...

LOUISIANA HOT BEANS (V)

Serves 4
Prep. 15 mins. Cook 50 mins.

300g/ 10½oz red kidney beans (dried or tinned)
1 large onion
4oz/100g bacon (leave out for vegetarian option)
2 cloves garlic
2 tabsp sunflower oil
2 fresh chilli's (any heat you like)
pinch of chilli powder
2 tabsp. tomato purée
salt and pepper
500ml / 18fl.oz hot chicken or vegetable stock
1 bunch spring onions

HOW to COOK

◊   Soak the beans over night in cold water.
◊   Drain and rinse well.
◊   Place in a large saucepan and cover with cold water, bring to the boil...
◊   Then cover and simmer for 1 hour... Or until the beans are soft...
◊   Peel the onion and cut the bacon in to small pieces and crush the garlic, heat a little oil in a large saucepan add the onions, bacon and garlic, fry for 2 minutes...
◊   Wash the chilli's, cut them in half, lengthways.
◊   Wearing rubber gloves, remove the seeds and chop the fresh chilli finely...
◊   Stir the chilli and tomato purée in to the onion mixture.
◊   Drain the beans, add the onion, bacon, garlic and chilli.
◊   Season with salt and pepper and a pinch of chilli powder (of your choice)
◊   Add the stock and bring to the boil, then cover and simmer for 40 minutes...
◊   Wash and trim the spring onions, slice in to rings... Check seasoning add more if needed
◊   Stir in spring onions, simmer for 5 minutes...
◊   Serve HOT! ...

This is a recipe I've used for a many years, another meal my Mum taught me and it's a regular in my house, with boiled rice and home made chapatis

TRADITIONAL CHILLI CON CARNE

Serves 4

20oz/500g minced beef
1 onion, finely chopped
2 garlic cloves, finely chopped
20oz/500g plum tomatoes, chopped
1 can red kidney beans, **drained and washed.***
2 tsp. chilli powder (medium heat)
1 tsp ground cumin
1 tsp. ground coriander
2 tabsp. plain flour
2 tabsp tomato puree
3 or 4 squares of 85% to 100% dark chocolate
2 tabsp. olive oil
½ pint /500ml. cold water

HOW to COOK

◊ Heat oil in a large frying pan or wok
◊ Add the onions, garlic and cook for 5 minutes
◊ Add the chilli, cumin, coriander, minced beef, stirring regularly, for around 5 minutes, or until the mince has browned
◊ Now add the tomatoes, tomato puree and kidney beans, stir in well.
◊ Add the dark chocolate, stir in well
◊ Add 500ml of cold water, stir in to the chilli mixture
◊ Reduce the heat and simmer for 25-30 minutes
◊ Heat the oven to Gas 4, 180C, 350F
◊ Place in an over proof dish or tagine
◊ Place in the oven for 20 minutes
◊ Serve with boiled rice or jacket potatoes, and grated cheese on top...

*NB

You must always wash and drain red kidney beans, before using, the liquid that they are stored in is very bitter...

TRADITIONAL CHILLI CON CARNE

Ingredients

Chilli con Carne

CAJUN PORK & BEEF BURGER'S

Makes 4-6 burger's
Prep. 20 mins. Plus 50 mins resting, Cook 20 mins.

8oz/200g. minced beef
8oz/200g. minced pork
1 onion, finely diced
2oz plain flour
1 egg
1 tsp. mixed herbs (dried)
6 tabsp. Henry's Ginger, Garlic and Cajun Mild sauce.
2 tabsp. sunflower oil for frying onions

HOW to COOK

◊ Combine the Beef and Pork mince, put to one side.
◊ Peel and finely dice the onion, lightly fry, until soft, let cool.
◊ Break egg into a bowl and whisk, until frothy.
◊ Now combine all the ingredients in one bowl, (mince, onion, egg, herbs, flour, sauce). Until well mixed mixed together. Cover with cling film and chill for 30 minutes.
◊ Once chilled, divide in to 6, tennis ball sized, balls, flatten and chill for another 20 minutes, then cook 2 at a time in a small frying pan, turning regularly...
◊ Serve these burgers hot... Best on a brioche bun with salad and onions...

TIP...

These can be cooked in one of three ways

Grilled

Fried or

Barbecued...

SMOKEY CHIPOTLE BEEF, WITH SWEET POTATO AND ONIONS

Serves 4

30oz/750g stewing steak (diced) or brisket (diced)
2 onions
1 medium sweet potato
2 heaped tabsp. smoky Chipotle rub (D C Sauces)
3 tsp lemon juice
1 pint cold water
1 beef stock cube
2 tabsp. soy sauce
3 tabsp. tomato ketchup
3 tabsp. white sugar
2 tabsp clear honey
3 tsp cornflour and water, mixed together.

HOW to COOK

◊   Place beef in a large dish
◊   Pour on the lemon juice, stir together so that the meat is covered evenly.
◊   Cover with cling-film, set on one side for **1 hour**
◊   Peel and slice onions
◊   Peel and diced, sweet potato
◊   Pour water in a large pan, add stock cube, onions, and sweet potato, put on a lid and bring to boil.
◊   Turn heat off add the beef and marinade juices, stir together.
◊   Add the honey, ketchup, sugar and soy sauce, and stir all together.
◊   Bring the pan back up to the boil,stir and reduce to a simmer.
◊   Simmer for **30** minutes, with the lid on the pan.
◊   Add cornflour at around **25** minutes, stir in well, bring back to the boil, to thicken up quickly...
◊   Serve hot, with rice or chucks of crusty bread.

CHICKEN TANDOORI MASALA GOUJONS

Serves 2

2 chicken breast
4oz/100g self-raising flour
¾ tabsp. salt
8 tabsps. olive oil
1 tabsp. tandoori masala powder
½ cup dry white wine or cider

HOW to COOK

◊ Cut the chicken breast in to thin goujons
◊ Mix the flour, salt and tandoori powder together on a plate
◊ Roll the chicken in the flour mix
◊ In a frying pan, heat the olive oil and a high heat for 2 minutes reducing to medium heat before adding the chicken.
◊ Cook 3 to 5 pieces of chicken at a time...Will take 5 -7 minutes for each batch
◊ Place on kitchen paper, to drain off excess oil...
◊ Serve HOT !

MARINADE

◊ Mix tandoori powder and white wine or cider together, pour over the chicken and marinate for 2-3 hours...

DIPPING SAUCE

LEMON AND JOLOKIA DIPPING SAUCE

4 Tabsp. Lemon juice
1 tsp. Bhut Jolokia sauce (DCSauce)
½ cup cold water
2 tabsp. white sugar
1 tsp. cornflower

◊ Place all ingredients in a large saucepan, except the cornflower, bring to boil, for 2-3 minutes
◊ Add the cornflower mixture, stir all together boil for 2-3 minutes and serve hot, with the goujons

SIDES

SPICY NEW POTATOES (V)

Serves 2
Prep. 15 mins. Cook 20 mins

500g of baby new potatoes, fresh or tinned
1 small onion (finely sliced)
2 cloves of garlic (finely sliced)
2 tabsp. sunflower oil
2 or 3 diced slices of cooked ham or bacon (remove for vegetarian option)*
2oz/ 50g grated cheddar cheese
12 twists of Daddy Cool's chilli salt
Optional vegetables : spinach, sweetcorn, broccoli

HOW to COOK

◊   Peel and sliced the baby potatoes (5mm) thick, put in a large pan, with water and boil for 15-20 minutes, or until soft. Drain and put on one side.

◊   Place the oil in a wok, and heat... Add the onions and garlic.

◊   Stir frequently to stop the sticking to the bottom of the pan... Add potatoes, cover for 5 minutes, then stir again

◊   Add other vegetables and ham/bacon if using... Stir together

◊   Cook until potatoes and onions are golden brown...

◊   Remove from the pan and place on serving dish, sprinkle with cheese, place under grill, until the cheese is bubbling and golden...

◊   I used 12 twists if Daddy's Cool salt mix... You can add more or less to your own liking...

◊   Serve hot...

*For the vegetarian option, leave out, ham and bacon

SPICY ONION & LEEKS

Serves 2

2 onions
1 leek,
1tabsp. sunflower oil
1, chicken stock cube
½ glass med. dry white wine
1, tsp Naga Sauce
1, tsp Reaper Ketchup 'KETCH the REAPER'
2, tsp. cornflour

HOW to COOK

◊   Slice the onion, and the leeks in to ¼" pieces
◊   Fry both in a little oil, until onions start to be translucent, crumble stock cube in to the pan and stir in, with the onions and leeks.
◊   Add half the wine to de-glaze the pan, keep stirring and add the Naga and Reaper sauces, add the rest of the wine and mix the cornflower with 2 tsp cold water, and add to the frying pan, to thicken the mixture.
◊   This make a very rich sauce and more white wine can be added to make extra sauce...

SWEET & SQUASHIE MASH

Serves 3-4
Prep. 20 mins. Cook 25 mins.

1 medium butternut squash
1 medium sweet potato
1 medium potato
1 tabsp. salted caramel sauce
3 tsp. Carolina Reaper sauce, 'Ketch the Reaper' (DCSauce)
2 tabsp. dark soy sauce

HOW TO COOK

◊ Peel and dice the butternut squash and sweet potato and potato, place in a pan of boiling water, boil until soft. (Around 20-25 minutes)
◊ Drain off the excess water, leave to cool for 5 minutes.
◊ Mash the vegetables together.
◊ In a bowl mix together the caramel,reaper and soy sauce, pour in to the vegetables and stir in well.
◊ The quantities listed give a fairly sweet side dish and less caramel sauce maybe added to suit the individuals taste.
◊ Serve hot, great with curries, chilli con carne and tandoori chicken.
◊ Also note that the reaper ketchup gets hotter with age so less may be required as the sauce matures.

AROMATIC FRIED RICE (V)

Serves 2
Prep. 10 mins. Cook 25 mins.

125g long grain rice (1, boil in the bag)
1 med. onion
2 chicken or vegetable stock cubes
1 tabsp. sunflower oil
1 tsp. turmeric
2 tabsp. Banana & Plantain Chutney (DCSauce)

HOW to COOK

◊   Boil the rice with one stock cube, until soft, and drain. (15 to 20 minutes)
◊   Chop onion roughly and fry, in the oil in a wok or large frying pan, add the second stock cube, and the drained rice, add the turmeric to the wok and stir, once an even colour is achieved stir in the 2 tabsp. of chutney, keep stirring, over full heat for 1-2 minutes or until any large chunks in the chutney are hot, and all flavours have combined, serve with chicken or sausages.

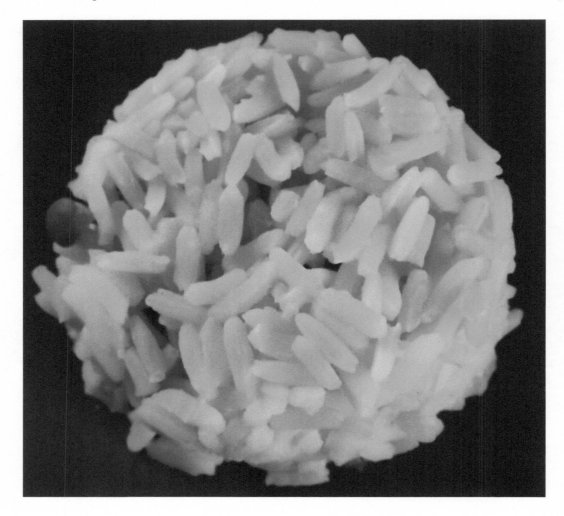

SARAH'S EGG FRIED RICE (V)

Serves 2-3
Prep. 5 mins. Cook 30 mins.

1 pint boiled water
2 cups basmati rice
2 chicken or vegetable stock cube
2 tabsp soy sauce
2 eggs
2 tabsp sweet chilli sauce
2 tabsp sunflower oil

HOW to COOK

◊ In a large pan add, water, 1 x stock cube and rice, Bring to the boil.
◊ Then reduce heat to a fast simmer, stir occasionally, do not let the pan boil dry, add more water if necessary
◊ Check rice after 20 minutes, the rice should be soft, remove from the pan, drain and set a side for frying.
◊ In a wok or large frying pan, add the oil and other stock cube, heat oil and stir in stock cube.
◊ Reduce heat to medium, add soy sauce, chilli sauce and eggs, stir in well.
◊ Make space in the middle of the rice and break the 2 eggs in to it, using a fork, whisk the eggs and stir in to the rice, continue to use the fork to keep the rice fluffy and keep stirring until the egg is cooked through
◊ Cover pan with a lid and cook for 5 minutes.
◊ Stir the rice mixture, to make sure it does not stick to the wok or pan.
◊ After 5 minutes the rice with be ready to serve.
◊ You can add more soy or chilli sauce if required.

JOHN'S SALT AND PEPPER CHIP'S (V)

Serves 2
Prep. 5 mins Cook 30 mins.

2 servings of chips, pre-cooked (25 mins.)
2 tabsp. sunflower oil
1 onion
2 or 3 sliced chilli's (red or green, dried or fresh)
1 chicken or vegetable stock cube
2 tabsp. passata
1 tabsp. sesame seeds
sea salt to taste.

HOW to COOK

◊ Heat the oil in a wok, on a high heat.
◊ Add the onions, fry until soft
◊ Add the stock cube, chilli's and passata.
◊ Stir the mixture on a medium heat, until the stock cube has dissolved completely
◊ Turn off the heat- add the chips to the mixture.
◊ Reheat the entire dish in the wok, for 2 to 3 minutes on full heat
◊ Transfer to a warmed serving dish, sprinkle with salt and sesame seeds

CHIPOTLE CUBED SPUDS

Serves 2-3
Prep. 10 mins. Cook 40 mins.

1Lb potatoes...
1 cup olive oil
3 tsp. smokey chipotle rub (DC Sauce)
1 Litre peanut or rapeseed oil... For deep frying

HOW to COOK

◊   Peel and cut the potatoes in to cubes. Boil for 15 minutes
◊   Heat oven to Gas 5
◊   Drain and dry thoroughly
◊   Heat the oil in a large pan on a high heat, then fry the potatoes until golden and crispy..
◊   Drain off excess oil, and place in an oven proof dish, keep the fried potatoes hot in the oven...
    15 mins.
◊   You may need to cook the potatoes in batches.
◊   Remove all the potatoes from the oven at the last minute, toss in the olive oil and sprinkle with
    the Chipotle rub... be quick...
◊   Then place the coated potatoes back in the oven for 5 minutes
◊   Serve this dish HOT ! .

SPICY POTATO PANCAKES

Serves 2-4
Prep. 15 mins. Cook 15 mins

1 ¾ Lbs/800g floury potatoes
1 large onion
3 eggs
3oz/75g sour cream
2 ½ oz/60g fresh white bread crumbs
2 tsp chilli rub (of your choice)
sea salt and pepper to taste
4 tabsps. Sunflower oil, for cooking

HOW to COOK

◊ Peel and wash the potatoes
◊ Grate, by hand or in a food processor. Squeeze out any excess water in a clean tea towel, then put them in a large mixing bowl.
◊ Heat oil on a large frying pan
◊ Peel and chop the onions, add with the bread crumbs, chilli rub to the potatoes.
◊ Lightly beat the eggs and add the to the mixing bowl, combine well
◊ Take 2 tablespoons of the potato mixture, for each pancake
◊ Place the potato mixture in the frying pan, 4-6 at a time
◊ Do not turn over until the edges are lightly browned (takes around 3 minutes)
◊ Keep each batch on a large plate in a low oven until all are cooked
◊ Serve hot

SERVING TIP

Ideal with kebabs, grilled sausages or bacon

CHILLI PIZZA DOUGH

Serves 2
Prep. 1 hr. Cook 20-25 mins.

6oz/150g rice flour
7oz/175g plain flour
2 tsp sea salt
1 tabsp. soft brown sugar
¼ oz/ 7g yeast (dried, active)
2 tabsp. sunflower oil
8 fl. oz. warm water
2 tsp chilli flakes or Rub (DCSauce or Henry's)

Extra plain flour for dusting work surface.

HOW to COOK

◊ Sift both flour's in to a large mixing bowl.
◊ Add the salt and sugar and oil.
◊ In a medium sized jug combine the warm water and yeast.
◊ Make a well in the centre of the dry ingredients, and pour in yeast liquid.
◊ Combine everything together to a smooth dough. A little more warm water maybe needed, to make the dough smooth.
◊ Now empty out the dough on to a flour
◊ Then return to the mixing bowl cover with cling film and set a side in a warm place for around 30 minutes, the d surface... And KNEAD for around 5 minutes. dough will raise up, and is then almost ready to use...
◊ Cut the dough in to quarters and knead each piece as required.
◊ Now light the oven Gas 5
◊ They can be square or round, pizza...
◊ Place on a baking sheet and rest for 10-15 minutes, the dough will rise up again, gently knock back down the dough and start to place on your coverings, anything you like... tomato, onion, ham, cheese, peppers etc...
◊ The oven should now be hot enough to bake your pizza..
◊ Place in the middle of the oven, the pizza take between 20 – 25 minutes to cook.
◊ They can be served HOT or COLD...

ONION AND MUSHROOM BAHJI

Serves 2
Prep. 10 mins. Cook 10 mins.

1 onion, finely chopped
4 medium mushrooms finely chopped
(Flour mix from tandoori masala goujons)
Plus
2 tabsps. self-raising flour
1 tabsp. smoky chipotle rub (DCSauces)
½ tsp salt
½ cup milk
1 egg
3 tabsp. sunflower oil

HOW to COOK

◊   Finely chop the onion and mushrooms
◊   Make batter, mix the flour, chipotle rub, salt, milk and egg together.
◊   Stir in the onions and mushrooms, this will become a thick batter
◊   In a small frying pan heat the sunflower oil on high for 2 minutes then reduce the heat slightly.
◊   Add a tabsp. of the mixture, cook for 2 -3 minutes on each side.
◊   Place on kitchen towel to drain of excess oil
◊   Serve HOT ! With chilli lager sauce, chicken goujons, rice or on there own with some mayonnaise...

DESSERTS

Shortbread is quick and easy to make, as I love sweet biscuit and spicy heat I wanted to see if they would work together and they did... The result is just perfect... Sweet, heat and spicy... You can also dip them in dark chocolate, that works well with the chillies too !

CHILLI SHORTBREAD

Makes 12-16 biscuits
Prep. 15-20 mins. Cook 20 mins + standing 10 mins

4oz/100g unsalted butter
2oz/50g soft brown sugar
6oz/150g plain flour
1 chilli, very finely sliced and seeds removed... I use "Medina" chillies when I can...
(you can make this recipe with mild, medium or hot chilli's) the choice is yours.
OR Jamokie sauce 3-4 tsp.
1 tabsp. sunflower oil.

HOW to COOK

◊ Preheat oven Gas4 / 180C. Line a large shallow baking tray with greaseproof paper, lightly oil, paper, set on one side.
◊ Cream butter and sugar together add chilli flakes.
◊ Sift in flour, and mix together.
◊ Empty dough on to a flour surface and knead, lightly.
◊ Roll out dough to roughly the size of the baking tray... push dough out to the edges.
◊ Prick all over the dough with a fork.
◊ Bake for 15 to 20 minutes or until golden brown. Remove from the oven, let the biscuit stand in the baking tray for 10 minutes, before removing to a cooling rack (leave on the greaseproof paper) until cold.
◊ Slice and store in an air tight container for up to two weeks.
◊ If you use fresh chillies, you will notice after a few days that the chillies will go slightly chewy... And you get more chilli flavour and heat too !

CHILLI CHURRIOS

Makes 8
Prep. 15-20 mins. Cook 5-10 mins.

1 batch chapati dough (see page 64)
2 tabsp. salted caramel sauce
2 tabsp. dessicated coconut
2 tabsp. chopped almonds
2 tabsp. dark chocolate chips
1 ½ tabsp. Jamokie (DCSauce)
½ cup cold water
6 tabsp. sunflower oil

HOW to MAKE and COOK

◊ In a bowl place salted caramel sauce, coconut, almonds and chocolate chip in a bowl and mix together, this will form a thick paste.
◊ Roll out your chapati,to around 2mm thickness, round in shape, I cut around a 24cm plate.
◊ Wet the edge's with a little cold water.
◊ Place 1 heaped tabsp. of the paste at the base of the chapati, roll in to a cigar shape, folding edges. Seal with water.
◊ Heat sunflower oil in frying pan, shallow fry for 5 minutes turning as each side lightly lightly browned
◊ You'll need to make sure that the churos is properly sealed, as, when the paste warms up it becomes runny, and may leak out, which you do not want to happen..
◊ Serve hot, with a sprinkling of icing sugar and a tabsp. of clotted cream or ice cream

A spicy twist on an old family recipe... I always remember my Mum's syrup sponge puddings so I used that to start with and came up with this recipe... I think it works really well together... Sweet, sticky and salty caramel sauce and a gentle warming heat from the jamokie sauce... And great with vanilla ice cream... and maybe a drizzle of jamokie sauce over the top...

CHILLI CARAMEL SPONGE PUDDING

Makes 2
Prep. 20 mins. Cook 20-25 mins.

3 eggs
6oz self-raising flour
6oz light brown sugar
6oz margarine (softened)
5 heaped tabsp. salted caramel sauce
2 tsp. Jamokie (DC Sauces)

HOW to COOK

◊   Light oven at Gas 5
◊   In a large bowl place the flour, sugar and softened margarine.
◊   In a small bowl, crack and beat the eggs together add them to the mixing bowl, beat all the ingredients together, until a smooth batter.
◊   On a baking tray place 4, ½Lb pudding bowls and, lightly grease with margarine
◊   In a small bowl combine the caramel sauce and jamokie
◊   Place 2 tabsps. Of the sauce at the base of each pudding bowl and then fill each bowl up to 2.5cms from the top of the bowl
◊   Place the baking tray with the bowls on in the centre of the oven
◊   Bake for 15 to 20 minutes or until golden brown on top
◊   When cooked, remove form the oven, let stand for 5 minutes.
◊   Serve with a scoop of vanilla ice cream

◊   If you don not like salted caramel sauce then just use plain caramel sauce, as this recipe works well with that too ! I know because I tried it !

CHILLI COOLEY'S

12 small sweet peppers or very mild chillies
2 pints sunflower oil, for deep frying
300 ml double cream, whipped to stiff peaks
2 tabsp. white sugar
icing sugar to garnish

BATTER

1 egg
1 cup semi-skimmed milk
1 cup plain flour

CHOCOLATE COATING

1 100g bar dark chocolate 85%
4 crushed glacé mints

HOW to COOK

◊ Remove stalks,tops and deseed peppers
◊ Pour oil in to a large, deep pan, heat on high for 5 minutes
◊ Make the batter, put all the ingredients in a large bowl and whisk together, this will be a very thick batter, which you will need to coat each pepper.
◊ Dip each pepper in to the batter.
◊ Place the battered pepper in to the oil, around 4 at a time.
◊ Fry until golden brown, remove from pan and let drain on several layers of kitchen paper and, to cool down, around 10 minutes.
◊ Melt the chocolate, 2 mins in a microwave or 5 mins. Over a pan of hot water.
◊ Stir in the crushed mints
◊ Dip each pepper in the chocolate and mint mix place on grease proof paper until set, you can do this in the fridge, takes around 15-20 minutes or top of the freezer for 10 minutes.
◊ Then pipe in the cream until each pepper in full of cream.
◊ Can be served straight away, or placed in the fridge until needed..
◊ These can also be frozen for up to 1 month...

SNACKS

One of my favourite snacks has to be cheese on toast but, I wanted to add a little heat to spice it up... So out came the collection of chilli sauces and cheese's and this one won... ' No Smoke Without Fire' works so well with a good mature cheddar...

You can use what ever cheese you like and for that matter any chilli sauce... But for me this combination is a winner !

THE ULTIMATE WELSH RAREBIT-HENRY !

2 slices bread, white or brown
2oz/50g mature cheddar cheese (grated) or (a cheese of your choice)
1 tabsp. Worcestershire sauce
4 tabsp. milk
2 tabsp. Henry's, 'No Smoke Without Fire' sauce
sea salt and pepper to taste.

HOW to COOK

◊ Light the grill
◊ In a bowl mix together the grated cheese, milk, Worcestershire sauce and Henry's sauce.
◊ Toast the bread on one side
◊ Remove from the grill and put on a chopping board, toasted side down.
◊ Place 2 -3 tabsp. of the mixture in the centre of each slice of toast, and spread this out to the edges.
◊ Place back under the grill, cook until the cheese is melting and bubbling and starting to turn golden brown...
◊ Remove from the grill... And serve...
◊ You can eat this hot or cold...

MUSHROOM BITES

Serves 2
Prep. 10 mins. Cook 5 mins.

8 medium sized Mushrooms
4oz/100g grated parmesan
1oz plain flour
1 tabsp. Henry's BBQ rub
2 eggs
½ tsp sea salt
½ cup sunflower oil for frying

HOW to COOK

◊   Slice mushroom, in to quarters
◊   Whisk eggs in a bowl
◊   Mix parmesan, plain flour, salt and BBQ rub in a separate bowl
◊   Dip each piece of mushroom in the egg then the dry mixture, let stand for 2-3 minutes
◊   Heat oil in the large frying pan or wok, on a high heat, turning down to ¾ heat when cooking the mushrooms
◊   Place 3-4 coated mushrooms in the frying pan or wok at a time..
◊   They take around 3-5 minutes to fry...
◊   Remove from frying pan on to kitchen towel, to drain of excess oil...
◊   Best served hot, as a starter or snack

Great for a starter or and evening snack, serve with a little mayonnaise

Quick to make, best eaten hot...

Quick and easy to make flatbreads. Great with a curry or chilli, can also be used with dips etc.

CHAPATI

Makes 8-10
Prep. 15 mins. Cook 5 mins. each

30oz/750gms chapati flour
1 or 2 tsp sea salt
½ cup sunflower oil or melted butter
250ml. tepid water, added as needed...

HOW to MAKE the DOUGH

◊   Place the flour,salt in a large mixing bowl and combine together...
◊   Add the oil or fat, rub in to the dry ingredients, to form a fine bread crumb...
◊   Gradually add a little water, and using a knife, start to stir and combine the mixture, keep adding the water in small amounts, until you can make the bowl, clean with the dough...
◊   Lightly flour a work surface and turn the dough out on to this and knead for 5 minutes.
◊   Stretch (knead) and pull the dough, to get the gluten working.
◊   Roll the dough in to a 3" diameter sausage shape, pull the ends gently, if the dough springs back, it is ready to use...

HOW to COOK

◊   Divide the sausage in to 10 equal pieces...
◊   Shape in to rounds, and roll out in to discs 3 ½ to 4mm in thickness...
◊   Approximately 9" in diameter...
◊   These chapatis are dry cooked...
◊   Heat a medium sized frying pan on a high heat...
◊   Add the chapati, turning regularly, cook each chapati until, golden brown patches appear on the surface, around 5 minutes each...

N.B

The dough will look wet at first, when in the frying pan, as it cooks golden brown patches will appear on the surface of the chapati... When it looks dry it is ready to serve, these can be kept warm in a low oven, before eating...

BEST SERVED HOT

PURIS

Makes 8
Prep. 10 mins. Cook 3-5 mins. each

4oz/100g chapati flour
4oz/100g plain white flour
1 tsp. sea salt
4 tabsp. melted butter
100ml / 3½ fl. oz warm water

HOW to MAKE the DOUGH

◊ Place flour and salt in a bowl.
◊ Add the oil and enough warm water to make a stiff dough
◊ Turn the dough on to a floured surface and knead for 5 minutes.
◊ Or until smooth and elastic.
◊ Place the dough in a clean bowl, cover with a damp cloth and let stand for 1 hour.
◊ Divide the dough in to 14 equal portions.
◊ Roll each portion in to a disc 10cm/4" in diameter

HOW to COOK

◊ Heat a little oil in a frying pan...
◊ Add one disc at once...
◊ Cook on a high heat for 3 minutes, flipping regularly, until the puri, puffs up and is golden brown and crispy...
◊ Remove from the frying pan and drain off any excess oil, serve **HOT.**

FIRE DEPARTMENT : FORWARD :

Cooking with and tasting chilli's from the mildest to the hottest, delivers ever increasing amounts of Capsiasin to the palette...

As Capsiasin is acidic, the best way to put the fire out is with copious amounts of alkaline, drinks or food...

So things like :

milk
yoghurt
cream
mint tea
cream crackers
are all ideal for this, purpose...

So for all those wondering why there is a fire department in a cook book, This is where we put the fire (heat) out...

As well as those I've suggested above here are a few more foods you can use :

celery, with cream cheese
cucumber
tomatoes
apple
lentils
lettuce...

All these will help calm the fire (heat) down...

CAN YOU BEAT THE ROLL

1 pack ready made shortcrust pastry
1Lb plain pork sausage meat
½ tsp mixed herbs, dried
1 egg, for egg wash
chilli sauces in varying heats or fresh chilli's of varying heats

Chilli's

Mild – Bell Pepper, red, green, yellow or orange (which ever you prefer)
Medium – Jalapeño
Medium – Tabasco
Hot – Scotch Bonnet
Hottest – Carolina Reaper

HOW to MAKE

◊   Roll out the shortcrust pastry to around 4mm think 30cm long and 20cm wide
◊   In 6 small bowl place a 3 tablespoons of the sausage meat in each one...
◊   In the first bowl add the mixed herbs, mix well in to the sausage meat
◊   In the second bowl add finely chopped bell pepper, mix in well to the sausage meat...
◊   Do the same in each bowl of sausage meat, making each one a little bit hotter.
◊   Now place a tablespoon of each mix down the centre of the left had side of pastry, leaving a gap in between
◊   Wet the edges of the pastry, fold the right hand side over the left, press down the edges with a fork to seal them...
◊   Press the pastry together between each spoonful of sausage meat... Mark the hottest with an 'X'
◊   Place on a baking tray, and coat with egg wash.
◊   Place in centre of the oven, back for 25-30 minutes, checking that the sausage meat is cooked, if not return for 5 -10 more minutes until cooked...

I wanted to do a fun recipe, so, I came up with this, a sausage roll that gets hotter as you eat it... From the mild red pepper to Carolina Reaper... and it works so well...

So this is basically a sausage roll with varying heats of chilli... You can use fresh chillies or sauces for this recipe, for fresh I chose jalapeño, scotch bonnet and Carolina reaper... and sauces I would you either a range of Daddy Cools (Ketch the Reaper) or Henry's Hot sauces (No Smoke without Fire)...

I get my sausage meat from my local butchers, Will's of Sandbach, Cheshire.

ATAY BIL NA'NA' – MINT TEA

Serves 4-6
Prep. 10 mins. Brewing time 10 mins.

1 Bunch Fresh Spearmint
2 tsp. Chinese Gunpowder Green Tea
2 tabsp. White Sugar, or to taste

HOW to BREW

◊ Cut the ends off the mint, leaving the leafy sprigs. Wash well, and shake dry wrap in a tea towel, to remove any excess water...

◊ Warm up your teapot, with some boiled water. Remove the water after 5 minutes, re-boil the kettle and fill the teapot half full with boiled water...Adding the green tea...

◊ Take a handful of the mint sprigs, crush them lightly and add to the teapot...Add more crushed mint sprigs until the teapot is three-quarters full, Add the sugar and fill the teapot with boiling water... let stand for 3 minutes...

◊ Pour out a glass of tea and pour it back into the teapot, repeat this twice... This will mix the tea and dissolve the sugar...

◊ Serve in tea glasses, pouring from a height to aerate the tea.

◊ Add an uncrushed mint sprig to each glass...

A SPECIAL
THANK YOU TO THE FOLLOWING PEOPLE

JOHN THOMPSON, my husband, best friend, for his love,support and lot's of encouragement...

STEVE COOLEY, amazing sauces and support

SHAWN OVERTHROW, awesome sauces and encouragement

PASCAL D'NARGEL, photographs of chillies, from around the world

STEVE YOUNG, for just being there...

CRAIG G. SMITH, for being there, when I needed an idea...

ERICA JADE, for getting this book published

WILL'S BUTCHERS for the sausagemeat

LLITTLE CHILLI SHOP the best chilli honey

DADDY COOL'S SAUCES

sauces, rubs and much more

HENRY'S SAUCE

sauces, powders, rubs, chutneys

Devil's Dynamite

chilli pastes

Little Chilli Shop

chilli honey

Will's Butchers,

sausagemeat

HENRY'S HOT SAUCE'S
AND
RUB'S

CHILLI & SAUCE SUPPLIERS

THE BACK GARDEN CHILLI NURSERY
T: +44 (0) 7513 131699
E: st27993@gmail.com

Daddy Cool's Chilli Sauce
T: +44 (0) 7583 403560
E: info@daddycoolschillisauce.co.uk
W: www.daddycoolschillisauce.co.uk

HENRY'S HOT SAUCE
T: +44 (0) 7969 243212
E: shawn.overthrow@yahoo.co.uk
W: www.henryshotsauce.co.uk

WILL'S BUTCHER'S
T: 01270 762015
Unit A, Market Hall, Sandbach, CW11 1AY

The Little Chilli Shop
T: 01248 810077
W: www.littlechillishop.com

Boston Ballistic Hot Sauces USA
T: +1 508-821-6999
www.bostonballistichotsauce.com

INDEX :

Tandoori Paste 32
Thank You's 71
Tomato Purée 32,39,40
Tomato Sauce 27,31,32,40,43
Traditional Chilli con Carne 40,41

Ultimate Welsh Rarebit 63

Worcestershire Sauce 63

'XXX' Lamb, Chicken or Beef Marinade